From Drug Dealer
to Disciple

From Drug Dealer to Disciple

My Journey of
Healing and Deliverance

Bryn Edwards
With Shelley Wilburn

From Drug Dealer to Disciple
My Journey of Healing and Deliverance

ISBN
Print: 979-8-9991659-0-9
eBook: 979-8-9991659-1-6

Edited by Shelley Wilburn, Walking Healed Ministries and Mountain Joy Publishing
Cover Art by Paul Ruane
Chapter Title Graphics by Gordana Stanisic from Pixabay

Published by That's My King Publishing

Printed in the United States of America

I have spent most of my sixty-one years in church and I know the power of God. I also spent many years in law enforcement, and I saw the evils of drug and alcohol abuse. I saw how it destroys lives and families. When I met Bryn and his wife, and heard a little of their story, I was amazed and hungry to hear the truth of what had happened in Bryn's life. I was so excited when I read the story; I laughed, and I cried. Once again, I am amazed at the power and forgiveness of God. What a great book and amazing testimony from a true man of God.

– Don Wilburn,
Owner, D.A. Wilburn Construction, Chaplain at Franklin County Sheriff's Dept., and Pastoral Minister at Purpose House Church

Table of Contents

Dedication i

Foreword.. ii

Introduction iv

1 In the Beginning 1

2 Making the Connection 8

3 No Such Thing as Luck 14

4 God, Help Me! 19

5 Savior, But Not Lord................................. 23

6 Cleaning Up.. 32

7 "Why Do You Fear?".................................. 40

8 Can We Skip the Big Fish?........................... 45

9 Sorcerer, Pagan, and then Revelation................. 50

10 I Know What I am Not 57

Appendix A — Jesus Wants to Work in You, Too 64

Appendix B — What is Tommy John?................... 67

Appendix C — About the Cover 69

Endnotes 71

About the Author 74

Dedication

I dedicate this book to my beautiful blessing of a wife, and so much more, Blayn, who has been with me on the mountain tops and in the valleys. Through the tears, the times of laughing, and everywhere in between, you stayed, and I thank God for you. I also dedicate this to my amazing children, Quynn and Banner, with whom God has blessed me abundantly, and has given new purpose to my life. I love you all deeply.

To anyone who has ever felt stuck in addiction. May you find the healing and deliverance God has shown to me.

Foreword

It is with great enthusiasm and a heart full of admiration that I pen this foreword for Bryn Edwards' transformative book, "From Drug Dealer to Disciple." In these pages, Bryn takes us on a compelling journey—a journey not only of personal redemption but also of profound purpose and faith.

As a dedicated member of the Purpose House Church community, I have had the privilege of witnessing Bryn's remarkable transformation. His story defies conventional expectations and shines a light on the power of grace, perseverance, and the transforming power of Holy Spirit.

From the shadows of a troubled past to the forefront of ministry, Bryn's progress has been nothing short of inspiring. Each step he has taken is a testament to the strength of his character and the call he felt to serve others.

Bryn's passion for his new path is palpable. He exudes a sense of purpose that is both contagious and uplifting. He reminds us that no matter where we begin, it is our choices and our willingness to embrace the changes that define our journeys. His story serves as a beacon of hope for anyone who has ever felt lost or alone in their struggles.

As you turn the pages of this book, you will find not just a narrative of transformation, but also a guide to understanding the values of compassion and forgiveness. Bryn encourages us to embrace our vulnerabilities, learn from our pasts, and ultimately, to seek out our true purpose. His insights are not only profound but also practical, urging readers to reflect and take action in their own lives.

I invite you to dive into Bryn's story with an open heart and mind. May you find inspiration, encouragement, and a deeper understanding of the power of redemption through his words. Bryn has truly become an integral part of our ministry, and I have no doubt that his journey will touch your life just as it has enriched ours at Purpose House Church.

With gratitude and anticipation,

Jason McKinnies
Senior Pastor
Purpose House Church

Introduction

No one wakes up one morning and decides, "Today, I'm going to become a drug addict!" Yet, that's where I ended up. It didn't happen overnight. Incidentally, neither did my deliverance.

In retrospect, God had been chasing me for many years, and I kept rejecting Him. But He was relentless.

Looking back on my life, God has given me revelation about all the times He called to me, then protected me when I rejected Him.

This speaks to His goodness, His love for us, His grace, and His mercy, which I guess may be more so. Mercy before you're saved, right? Because we don't get what we deserve, and then we are saved by grace through faith in Jesus.

I look back now, and I see His mercy. I see it in all the times He had His hand on me when I was as far away from Him as I could possibly be; from being drunk and wrecking my truck, it launching into the air, bouncing off a culvert and getting stuck twenty feet off the road, never touching the tree line (which I completely missed), to wrecking motorcycles, flipping on the pavement, end-over-end like a rag doll, being launched in the air, and only cracking my helmet on the side. Yet never getting seriously hurt.

Time after time, God kept me from harm. Time after time, He tried to draw me in. And time after time I rejected Him.

I'm not mad or upset at the point I had got to. I could have easily laid blame where blame didn't exist. *I* was the one who kept rejecting God, yet He kept trying to reach me. He kept chasing me.

Sometimes, things just have to get bad enough and a person has to get to the end of their rope before they finally realize something has to give. That something and someone was me.

I look back now and I'm grateful for all the times God tried to draw me in, even though I rejected Him, and He never gave up on me.

I wasn't aware of it until after my deliverance when I looked back. Hindsight is 20/20, and God gave me a clear picture.

I never thought I would write a book about my experience with drugs, nor my deliverance, until I was sitting in a writer's coaching session working on a different book, and my coach spoke up and said, "I think you need to tell your story first."

She then explained to me the importance of getting my deliverance story out there so maybe someone else who may be struggling with addiction, or whatever may be controlling them, can see that God loves them and is as relentless in pursuing them as well. That's when I realized it was time.

What you're about to read is my journey from how I got involved in drugs, to how God delivered me from it all in such a way that I'll never be the same again.

1 In the Beginning

Growing up wasn't so bad. Both of my parents were great people. They still are! They're also still married. So, I didn't deal with divorced parents, or a broken home. My brother and I never lacked for anything. Our parents raised us well.

As far as church goes, we may have gone to church here and there, but we weren't consistent, per se. We may have gone more than I remember from when I was younger, but I do remember we were mainly in and out through my grade school years.

When I was younger, I do remember going through Confirmation in the Methodist Church. I also started doing travel baseball during the summer, so sports started to take precedence over going to church.

Of course, then there was Christmas and Easter.

Overall, my brother and I were well cared for and loved by both parents. Our lives were good. So, how did I end up into drugs?

I don't fault my parents for any of this. Not the sporadic church attendance, nor my slide into drugs and alcohol.

I look back and think, man, how cool would it have been to have been raised in church? But on the other side of the coin, I'm also very thankful and grateful that we weren't. It might sound weird, but when I came to the church we're in now, I didn't have any preconceived notions or any rigid religious strongholds, mindsets, or beliefs, that needed to be broken. I was just able to allow God to move upon me and hear Him, as well as allow the Spirit to speak to me. I didn't have any walls that needed torn down so they could be built back up. It was just a clean slate. I was a clean slate.

But I digress.

Initially, my family wasn't that into church. Like I said earlier, whenever I got into sports, that took precedence, and church became a twice a year thing.

As such, I was about to take a journey into the dark world of drugs and alcohol. Of course, back then it didn't look like that to me. It merely looked like experimenting, fitting in with the crowd, partying, and it took off from there.

As with any teenage boy, I guess, I began chewing (tobacco) when I was around fourteen. On my fifteenth birthday, though, I tried alcohol for the first time. That's when I also got drunk for the first time.

After that, I didn't drink every weekend, but here and there throughout high school. That led to more and more frequently, which led into drinking on weekends.

I didn't really do any drugs in high school. Maybe in my senior year I might have smoked pot a couple of times, but all in all, it was just the drinking heavily and partying.

Growing up, many people say things like, "Oh, they're in high school," and then they downplay it to, "They'll grow out of it."

I heard a statement somewhere that says, *Where you start partying is where you stop maturing.* This basically means that at whatever age a person begins drinking, doing drugs, etc. that's where they stop maturing mentally, maybe emotionally, too.

It made me think and suddenly, some puzzle pieces started fitting together. I don't know the science behind that, but I'm sure there's some sort of scientific explanation.

In high school I played baseball and football. I must have been good because I got a baseball scholarship, which plays into part of what God later showed me in being saved. I'll get to that in another part of the book.

Ironically, the baseball scholarship was to a Christian college. However, that summer I had a partial torn ligament in my elbow. I believe they called it *Tommy John*[*].

The doctor said I could do rehab if I didn't want to have surgery. I opted to do rehab and part of it would happen when I was at college. But at this point, through some friends, I had gotten into smoking weed. I was smoking quite a lot of it and at a Christian college, obviously, you're not exactly supposed to do stuff like that.

My elbow really didn't bother me unless I was throwing a baseball and since I didn't want to have surgery, I decided I was done with it. Also, part of it was because I just wanted to party. That wasn't the case at school. No partying.

At school, I would leave my dorm room, go to the parking lot, sit in my car and smoke weed by myself. Then, I would go back to my room.

After a week, I decided to leave college and I came back home. I wouldn't go back to school.

Since I hadn't gone back to the Christian college, or even a different college, I started partying more, drinking more, and smoking more weed. This would last for quite a few years.

~

In my twenties, I started working at bars. I did that for a couple of years. It was the kind of life I was living and the people I was running with, so why not work in it? During that time, I had moderately gotten into bodybuilding.

I had moved to Florida and while living there, I began bodybuilding more intensely. This led me to start using steroids.

In order to bulk up, steroids helped. In addition, I

also took HGH (Human Growth Hormones), as well as insulin.

I used steroids on and off for quite a while and ended up manufacturing them. I would sell those and discovered I made pretty good money from it. But at one point I stopped manufacturing and just ordered from overseas and sold them that way.

I became an entrepreneur. I've heard it said that some guys inherit the family business. In my life, there was no family business... I made my own. Looking back, between the ages of eighteen and twenty-seven, I pretty well had a non-taxable income.

Also, at eighteen, I got my first tattoo. If you've seen me, you understand this statement about getting a tattoo. There is a story behind even all the tattoos, which I will explain later.

~

Now, things in the bars could be rowdy. And due to some of those things, I didn't stay in the bars for long and left soon after. Frankly, I just didn't want to get stabbed. I did still have morals.

I lived in Florida for a year, then moved back to Illinois, where I decided that bodybuilding was something I could really get into.

When I had left the bar scene, I went full bore into bodybuilding. If I was going to do it, I decided I was in it to win it.

I was still using substances: steroids, HGH, insulin, but I had periodically stopped using cocaine (I'll get to that in a minute). My usage was intense for around four years. It was in those four years that I was sober. I wasn't even drinking.

At one point I was 295-pounds with eight-pack abs. My body fat percent was extremely low, five percent or less. I was very regimented with all my supplements and all my food.

During that time, I was regimented, very committed, to bodybuilding. I had coaches I paid. I ate what they told me to eat. I did what they told me to do. I worked out as they told me to work out and even did cardio. I didn't deter from the plan. Therefore, I understood discipline, which I believe is what eventually helped me spiritually. I understand discipline, and not in a legalistic form.

I was living by myself in Florida, but it was lonely, so I decided to move back home. When I moved back to Illinois, I had started hanging out with some people who were drinking a lot and smoking weed, and I started using cocaine. I did that because I didn't want the calories from the alcohol. I reasoned in my mind, cocaine didn't have calories, so that would work for me.

What was really happening was that I needed a fix. To get that fix, I had to pick something different. Therefore, the choice was cocaine.

Over time, I came to a point where I needed to stop bodybuilding. Anyone who looked at me would think I was a very healthy person. I wasn't. Yes, I was lean. I was big and muscular. But I was unhealthy. My blood pressure was high, I would get out of breath even putting on my shoes or even putting on my seat belt in the car. I could barely reach across my chest to grab the seatbelt.

You may be thinking, I can see where tying your

shoes would be difficult, having to bend down or bend over. Let me explain.

I was doing forty-five minutes of cardio, seven days a week. I would hit the high intensity training on cardio on the treadmill, so I should not have been out of breath putting on shoes. I didn't even tie my shoes. They were slip-ons. Therefore, getting out of breath putting on shoes shouldn't be happening.

That's when I decided to stop bodybuilding. I had burn-out. In truth, I was just wanting to party again. I knew from experience, you can't effectively do both, and if I'm going to do something, I'm doing it all-in.

Plus, with the bodybuilding, I was getting to an unhealthy point. I knew that to be competitive and where I wanted to be, I would have had to put on another forty pounds. I just didn't want to go there. It was unhealthy.

Granted, I knew that drinking and doing drugs are unhealthy, but in my mind, that's where I was. I also knew drinking and drugs were counterintuitive to bodybuilding, so bodybuilding went.

I started going out with friends again, drinking some and doing a little cocaine here and there. In the beginning, I didn't do it that much, because I still had that bodybuilding mentality. However, it got progressively more and more… and more.

Since I knew some people in Florida, I had the bright idea: Hey, this is the best business plan ever! If I sell cocaine, then I don't have to pay for cocaine. Then I'll always have cocaine to do!

And this is how I became a drug dealer.

2 Making the Connection

After my bright idea about getting into dealing, I made some connections, made a few calls, and set it up. I would drive down to Florida, pick up some cocaine and drive it back to Illinois. I tried to be strategic and would choose the longer weekends, or holiday weekends like Memorial Day or Labor Day weekend to make my pickups. It was a good drive.

I did that back and forth for a while. I was distributing decent quantities, and using, which was mostly on the weekends.

Eventually, I got connected with someone who was more local. This way, I wasn't having to drive as far or plan out trips as much, and it was more readily accessible.

I started doing trips every other week. Distribution increased and therefore, so did my usage. Let me add, it wasn't the little nickel-and-dime stuff.

After nearly two years, my usage progressed, and distribution stalled. Even though it was a fair amount, it wasn't progressing. I wanted more.

When I started with the more local connection. I was told, "Once you're on payroll, you're on payroll." I knew what that meant. I mean, it's their money. It's their business. Essentially, it's their livelihood. In that world, money talks and that's what it's all about. So, I knew that meant once you say yes to being on payroll, you're on payroll and you don't get off payroll.

I knew that if I ever wanted to get off payroll, there was some form of repercussion that was going to happen. Money is the motivator in the drug world. Therefore, when money decreases, there are repercussions. Someone has to pay.

It was around this time that I met up with the woman who would become my wife. Blayn.

Of course, we had known each other in high school, but we didn't exactly run in all the same social circles.

During our high school years, we would see each other at school, obviously, and some sporting events, even some parties. After high school, we would sometimes see each other at bars or other parties.

Now, years later, we reconnected at a bar and ended up talking. I was having some people over after that and she came over. We started hanging out. Afterwards, we started dating. It wasn't long before we were engaged, and soon married.

And I was still using and dealing drugs.

I can't really say I had my usage under control. Does anyone really? But it had become minimal and only on the weekends after Blayn and I were together. However, the usage, though minimal, meaning I didn't do it often, but the amount I did was large, and had increased to a point where I would be high and awake for five or six days at a time. Then I would crash and sleep for a day.

Blayn saw all of it.

Somewhere along this time, I had developed what doctors call *sleep paralysis*. Looking back now, the doctors can call it whatever they want. Sleep paralysis is where you have a demonic attack on you, while you're asleep.

My eyes would be shut but my mind would be awake. I would lay there, and I couldn't breathe. It was as if I was being choked. I couldn't say anything, I couldn't move, yet I was awake and completely defenseless. It was completely and one-hundred-percent demonic... and terrifying.

Imagine someone choking you but you can't do anything about it, yet you still know everything that's going on. It's like being trapped in your own body. You're a prisoner and the prison is *you*.

When I would finally be able roll or flip off of the bed, or the couch, I would start gasping for air, nearly crying. It was horrible.

Blayn would see it and ask, "What's wrong?"

I would tell her, but it happened numerous times. Then, I would be up and couldn't go back to sleep.

Shadow People

I also started seeing things in the shadows and couldn't figure out what was going on. In the drug world they call them, *Shadow People*. It's usually brought on from being on drugs and being awake for days on end, almost like hallucinations. I've come to learn that in doing drugs, it opens you up spiritually.

Shadow People are really demons. In doing drugs and thinking you're just high, the door to the spirit realm is opened and it lets in the demons and the terrors that will torment you. That's why such crazy things happen around people who are using.

It's a combination of being high and then also being tired. Many people say, "Oh, you're just hallucinating." But that's not really the case. Those are demons you see walking around. It's terrifying. And I was being tormented by them.

"The thief does not come except to steal, and to kill, and to destroy." John 10:10, NKJV.

When I was younger, I once took hallucinogens and tried to go to sleep. Bad idea. I was laying on my bed and suddenly I saw the Grim Reaper in my room. I was scared to death and didn't move. Paralyzed with fear. I didn't do a thing. I barely breathed.

I lay there for what seemed like hours when, in reality, it was only for a couple of minutes or so. But I remember laying there, stiff, staring at it, trying to reason with it, in my mind, to just go away.

Of course, the enemy can't hear your thoughts, but at the time, I didn't know that. And since I was terrified, all my reasoning went on in my mind. At this point, I didn't understand the spiritual. I figured it was probably just a coat or something, to pacify and ease my mind. Then, just as suddenly, it went away. It was only there to torment me.

Back to the point.

We had found out that Blayn was pregnant and with all the sleep paralysis, staying awake for days, and seeing demons, I wanted to be done using drugs.

I was in this pretty deep. I wanted out, but I didn't know how to get out. I knew the repercussions. Still, I wanted to be done; done selling, done using, I wanted to be done. There are many reasons.

My motorcycle had been repossessed. Then, my car was repossessed. Our house would probably have been repossessed next, but fortunately my parents stepped in and kept us from losing it.

I couldn't take care of myself, let alone a wife – and throw a newborn into the equation and it didn't compute. I knew I was close to losing my job. I did have an outside job in addition to dealing and distributing, but I wasn't managing any of it very well.

Fortunately, my dad helped me. I knew I needed to do something different. I wanted to stop and one day it kind of hit head-on at my job. I was given a choice: do outpatient rehab or lose my job. I knew if I took a drug test, I would definitely lose my job, and I knew what would happen then.

I chose outpatient rehab. That turned out to be a joke.

In rehab they talk about drugs and alcohol. You go

in sober and talk about drugs and alcohol for three or four hours. Then when you leave, you want to go do drugs and drink alcohol. At least that's how I felt afterwards.

Rehab didn't help. I told them I needed help. I wanted more help than what was given. At this point, I wasn't going to church, either. But at rehab, when I cried out for help, all I was told was, "Oh, you're doing a good job. Just keep going."

What ended up happening was that I continued doing drugs, because I needed help and wasn't getting it. I just didn't know from where I needed the help.

I was exhausting all my options, all the ways in which I thought I could stop doing drugs. They all ended up leading me back to doing drugs.

I was honestly trying to stop using, but I was not yet at the point where I wanted to stop dealing, because I was concerned with the repercussions.

I don't know that I was afraid, necessarily. Although, at this point I really didn't care if I lived or died. I wasn't what you would call suicidal. I wasn't wanting to take my own life. But I also wasn't concerned if I died. That would be one way to get out completely. However, I would no longer be here; not for Blayn, and not for our baby who was on the way.

3 No Such Thing as Luck

Earlier, I talked about getting tattoos. My getting them is significant, but when I was getting them, it was just that, getting tattoos. I would later discover that God even used those tattoos in what He was about to do in me.

People have asked me if I thought tattoos were addicting. I think they're addicting to people for a couple of reasons. I believe some really like the art, and some tattoos are very beautiful. People sometimes have an arm, leg, or even their bodies covered with various tattoos, using a theme, for whatever reason.

I've also been asked about one tattoo having a

specific meaning. There were a couple that I did choose specifically, especially one I chose in memory of my grandma.

I got my first tattoo when I was eighteen, for my grandma, who had passed away when I was fifteen. It was a tribute to her.

My parents never wanted me to get a tattoo, so I broke it to my mother by saying it was for Grandma.

When I started getting more and more tattoos, I was in my early twenties. I knew my parents didn't want me to get any below my elbow, and since I was being rebellious and defiant, I went with my left hand first because, in theory, it broke the ice per se. Therefore, anything between my hand and my arm was fair game. I mean, I already had one on my hand! So, in my rebellious thinking, they really couldn't care about it now, although, at their request, I did honor not getting any on my face and neck.

In the beginning, I picked out my first couple of tattoos; on my hand and my fingers. Other than that, I let the tattoo artist pick. As of right now, I have over forty tattoos, and most of them were chosen by the tattoo artist. I'm not bragging about that. It's just the way it went. I would tell him if I had anything sentimental, that I would let him know, but other than that, I just wanted some cool tattoos.

Of course, back in that day, there were several choice words spoken. That's how we talked then. All of this is before healing, before deliverance, before Jesus.

The tattoo artist chose what he wanted and when I would show up, he would ask me what I thought about this tattoo. I would always say something like, "Cool! Let's do it!"

We often had themes going and he would do pieces that fit that theme. But none of my tattoos were because of any certain thing... except two specifically.

When I was bodybuilding, I got a tattoo on the palm of my hand that says, *No Such Thing As Luck*. While I wasn't a believer in Jesus at that time, I also didn't believe in luck. I believed you made your own luck. Therefore, entrepreneur that I was, I was out there making my own luck with what I was doing. In my mind it all made sense, especially when I was dealing.

After my salvation and deliverance, that tattoo took on a different meaning. There really is no such thing as luck. There are *blessings*. We are not lucky. We are *blessed*.

The second tattoo I chose I put on my middle finger. It was a circle with a line through it and the number twelve. In the drug world, twelve is referencing cops, and twelve is the narcotics division. Therefore, the circled twelve with a line through it was symbolic of what the drug world thinks of that. Need I say more?

After my deliverance, that tattoo is the only one I got covered. I have friends now who are in law enforcement. Not only did I not want that tattoo showing, but I also didn't want to offend anyone, or answer questions regarding the meaning of that tattoo.

Plus, I didn't want it on me anymore, so what I did then – even though it may sound counterintuitive – was to get tattoos on my other fingers to take away any attention from that tattoo; one is a cross, and they're all for Jesus.

There are people who get tattoos because they believe they're addicted to them, but deep down I believe there is an underlying issue for which they can't explain other than, "It's addicting."

In that time of my life, I was going every other week getting tattooed. Sometimes it would be for three or four hours, and up to six hours. One time I sat for nine hours straight. With all my tattoos, I sat from start to finish. I didn't do any of them in sessions. It was one and done, regardless of how long I had to sit there. Looking back, I guess one could say I was addicted to getting tattoos.

I didn't fully understand why they were addicting for me until 2024, after I had attended a men's conference.

The man preaching the conference had us all grab hands and begin praying over the scars for people who had been cutting themselves, doing self-harm. As we prayed, suddenly these scars started disappearing from people. I could see men looking down where their scars had been, feeling their arms, and freaking out because the scars were going away, and some were even gone! It was amazing to witness.

After I got back from the conference, and I was telling someone the story of the men whose scars were disappearing. I was reenacting their reactions as I told the story, and reached over and rubbed my arm. This was where I had some deep scars from one of my tattoos, when the artist went a little deep in outlining.

Suddenly, it occurred to me that I didn't feel the scars on my arm. It was smooth. That's when I realized even *my* scars were gone!

When I finished telling the conference story, I walked away, baffled over the disappearance of my tattoo scars. I was thinking, *God, what's going on?*

He said to me, *It was the same thing. You did it for the same reasons. It just looked different.*

I thought back to all those times I would say, "I'm so stressed out. I've got to get tattooed. I *need* to get tattooed." In my mind, it was my stress relief.

I was going every other week to get a tattoo. I called it my *tattoo fix*. Afterward, I would be okay for a while, but then I would be right back in there getting another one. In essence, I was cutting, but it wasn't I who was inflicting pain, or self-harm. I was paying someone else to do it.

After re-telling that conference story, when it all dawned on me what had taken place, God said, *Why do you think you haven't wanted to get another tattoo? It wasn't really because of money. It's because I delivered you from that.*

At the time, I didn't know it, but now that I do, God gave me that revelation and clearly delivered me. I now have a better understanding of why tattoos are addicting to some people.

4 God, Help Me!

"God is our refuge and strength, A very present help in trouble." – Psalms 46:1, NKJV

I believe that people who are in addiction really don't want to be there. As I said in the beginning, no one gets up one day and decides to be a drug addict. It happens slowly, over time. It's a slow fade; when a person has nothing else to do, or feels they have nothing else to live for, or it even happens because of prescription drugs. Regardless, I believe no one *decides* to become an addict.

In addiction, you're really feeding a demon. That demon eventually requires more... and more... and more… and even more. Before long, that's all you're doing, and you're not getting anything out of it like you once did when you first started using. It's no longer fun.

Isn't that how the enemy works? It's fun for a while, and then you realize you're in too deep. That's when the enemy whispers, *I've got you.*

I found myself at the lowest of lows. My world was crashing down around me. My wife was pregnant. I was still on drugs, drinking, and getting high.

The only reason I wanted to stop, or so I thought, was because I knew we had a baby on the way. God had other plans, though, which weren't revealed to me just yet. He was simply waiting for me to make my decision.

I was still selling, but also trying not to use. It was hard. When there are drugs in the house, it's difficult to stay away from them and not use them. However, it had started to decrease.

Since Blayn was pregnant, she was staying sober (her story is for another place and time). She had started attending church and had been asking me to go with her. Of course, I would act like I was asleep on the couch, when I really wasn't, just so I didn't have to go. She knew.

God was still working.

I really wanted to stop using, but I just wasn't sure what to do. I needed help.

It was while I was painting the nursery in preparation for our new baby when everything came crashing down around me.

I was on the floor, crying. I didn't know what to do. I kept thinking, what do I do? *What do I do?* I hated myself for how I had become. I was at the end of my rope. I had hit the bottom with nowhere else to turn. That's when I found myself crying out in the most informal way.

"God, help me!"

I didn't know what else to do. I fell face first on the floor, crying and saying, "God, help me!" because I had exhausted everything else I could think of.

That's when things started to change.

When I cried out, *God help me*, God helped me! Later, He took me back to that and showed me a bird's eye view of myself in that room.

As I was sitting there, I watched as demons were closing in on me. When I hit the floor and yelled out, Jesus came in and picked me up in His arms, like a little kid. The moment He did that, those demons left. That's when things in my life started to change.

~

A couple of weeks after that moment on the floor with Jesus, was Easter Sunday. I find it ironic. However, before this, whenever Blayn would ask me to go to church, I feigned sleep to keep from having to go. Not on this Easter.

This time, when she asked, "You want to go to church?" maybe that moment on the floor took me back to when I was a kid and just going here and there, I don't know. Maybe there had been some seed planted in me back then. It doesn't return void, right?

I believe God allowed me to get all this other stuff

out of me, out of my own ways of helping myself, exhaust all those options, and then let that seed come forth. Then, He let me remember going to church on Easter, as a little kid. That probably helped me say yes to Blayn about going to church that Easter, too.

Now that I think of it, that moment in the nursery with Jesus is ironic that it was in the nursery – because it was there where He picked me up like a little kid, and my life changed.

I never really thought of that, to connect those dots so-to-speak. However, this was the first service I had come to Purpose House Church (then Southern Illinois Worship Center).

And… if I told you I never did drugs again after that, I would be lying.

5 Savior, But Not Lord

"The LORD is my rock, my fortress, and my savior…" – Psalms 18:2a, NLT

Jesus saved me out of that situation when I cried out to Him, but my troubles weren't over… yet.

I was still selling drugs. My usage had decreased, but it was still there. But I was sick of even just doing it here and there. I didn't want to do it anymore. Period.

I told Blayn, "Hey, I'm done selling. Like, I'm *done.*"

Basically, I tried to do it my own way, and essentially, I wanted a Savior to save me from *using* drugs, but not be my Lord in leading me away from *selling* drugs.

In salvation, there's supposed to be two deaths; Jesus dying so we can live, but then we are supposed to die (to ourselves) so He can live in and through us. I was okay with Christ dying so I could live (Savior), but I wasn't ready to die to myself so He could live in and through me (Lord).

Then I realized I couldn't stop doing drugs and still sell drugs. I had had this moment with Christ where I cried out to Him, and things started to change.

I was wanting to stop using drugs altogether. The usage had significantly decreased, but I was out (of drugs), and I was glad I was out. It was a relief that I didn't have any drugs in the house, therefore I was done.

This is typically where I would go get more, but instead I had stacked up some cash and I called my supplier. I was going to tell him, "I need to talk to you." This was our code for, *I need to meet with you.*

I decided I would meet up with him, give him his money, and tell him I'm done.

I told Blayn, "Hey, I don't know what's going to happen after this, but if you want, you can go stay with my parents, or you can go stay with your family. I get it. I'm not mad at you if you do that. I'm not upset with you. You've got a baby on the way."

I said it before, when you're told you're on payroll, then you're on payroll. You don't get off. They own you. I didn't exactly know what was going to happen afterwards, but I wanted to make sure my wife, and unborn baby were safe.

Blayn said, "No. I'll ride it out with you."

So, I made the call. He was out of town. I waited for three or four months for him to return my call, but he never did. He never got in touch with me.

I had that money sitting there, but I never heard back from him. Then one day I saw a buddy who knew him, and I asked, "Hey, where is he? I need to talk to him because I was wanting to go give him the money and tell him I'm out, I'm done."

"Oh, you haven't heard?"

"No. What?"

"He got popped for a quarter-million-dollar transaction. He's going to prison."

It wasn't like I was wanting him to go to prison, but when I heard that, it was like an elephant came off my shoulders. It was a huge release.

You know, now that I know the Bible more, how many times did God go before His people and deal with things, so they didn't even have to?

I feel He got this out of the way so that I could get cleaned up. However, I couldn't just stop and be completely done. Addiction doesn't work that way. Yes, God can take it all away in an instant, but what would I have learned?

Every person is on their own journey. Every person must learn in their own way. God is still God. He is sovereign. He is holy. And He allows our path for reasons known only to Him. This was my path.

~

I still drank. Heavily. I guess, thinking back, I just switched from cocaine to more alcohol. It wasn't good. In my mind, though, I couldn't just go from that to nothing, because at this point, whatever about salvation, in my mind I was now safe.

I'm not here to debate whether I was or wasn't saved. I don't know; the fruit might not have been there all the way, because at that point, I was really wanting a Savior to save me from my negative situations and circumstances. However, I didn't want a Lord to lead me and direct me away from those situations, so I never had to go. Just direct me onto the right path.

I basically shifted from cocaine to alcohol because in my mind, that was okay because alcohol was legal and cocaine was not, so I was at least legal, in a worldly sense.

I was asked if I ever worry about things (or people) from my past coming back. No. I believe God went before me before I was really even faithfully following Him.

I believe there's a crying out in need of a Savior, where He starts to show you and do some things in your life. Then there's the difference in actually making Him Lord and *in* you, faithfully following Him in obedience. It's like putting down your will and crucifying your flesh and picking up His. If He protected me then, when I was only 50/50, how much more will He now?

Holy Spirit and Fire

On New Year's Eve of 2018, our daughter was born. I was still drinking heavily, but not using cocaine. At the end of that month, we were wanting to have her dedicated to the Lord. To do that, we had to do membership classes. We weren't yet members of the church, so we went to membership classes.

After that, we started serving, getting more into attending church, being regular... well, at least three weeks out of the month, anyway. For us, that was regular. We would slide in the back, then slide back out.

Once we started serving, we started getting plugged in with more people, connecting with them, and we started to kind of grow in the church, to blossom more.

My drinking was starting to slow down more, but only on the weekends. I was still drinking on the weekends, but throughout the week, I would drink heavily. I didn't want to be hung over and come to church.

I had some people who were telling me, "Hey, pray for baptism in the Holy Spirit."

I said, "Okay."

I really wanted to ask, "What is that?" At this point, I wasn't really reading my Bible. I wasn't really praying. Therefore, when I was told to pray for baptism in the Holy Spirit, I finally asked what it was.

They just told me to pray, just ask God for it.

I started praying. I was also listening to the Bible when I would do cardio, which, I'm not against listening to the Bible, but it doesn't work best for me. However, in the beginning of this journey, it was a foot in the door.

I was praying to be baptized in the Holy Spirit, not fully knowing or understanding what I was praying for. It was around 2020 now, and at this point I had given my life to Christ, I had said a more formal prayer of salvation and done all that.

I was diving in more to Him and some of the unfruitful things were fading away, slowly. I was getting more into serving and church things. Yet, I wasn't all the way in with Jesus. I was still teetering.

One day I had picked up our daughter from my parent's house and was driving home. I hadn't been on the road very long, and she fell asleep in the truck.

Suddenly, tears just started pouring out of my eyes. It's as if Holy Spirit suddenly overwhelmed me and tears started flowing down my face; huge, crocodile tears. I thought, I'm not sad! But I'm also not understanding what's happening. Suddenly, all I can do is pray and prophesy. I'm driving down the road, crying, praying, and prophesying and I couldn't stop.

When I got home, I got the baby out of the truck and took her in the house, and laid her on the couch, but I couldn't sit down.

I began pacing the house, breathing hard, praying, and prophesying, laying hands on my daughter, praying over her, prophesying over her, and then here I went again.

I kept thinking, *what is going on!* What is this?

I had no idea. I was the only one home with our daughter. She was asleep on the couch, and Blayn was at work.

Suddenly, it felt like something just bubbled up out of my stomach. I didn't know what was going on, so I didn't say anything. But then I know one hundred percent that I still received Holy Spirit in that moment.

Afterward, I couldn't sit down for another hour or so. I kept pacing the house, praying, and prophesying, and I kept looking at my hands wondering, *what in the world is going on!* Because it felt as if electricity was shooting through me.

I felt like, if I were to touch a dead flower it would come back to life! I really kind of wanted to find one because I knew if there had been one in the house, and I were to touch it, I believe that flower would come back to life! There's not a shadow of a doubt in my mind or my heart that that's what would have happened.

Some people might say, "Are you? Are you baptized in the Holy Spirit? You didn't pray in tongues, so you didn't."

I one hundred percent received baptism in the Holy Spirit. If I had not received it, it would have stopped right there. But it continued afterwards, and I couldn't sit down for another hour-and-a-half even after that.

I believe people get baptized in the Spirit differently. God speaks to them. There's not a one-size-fits-all, because I know people who have had this overwhelming peace just flood over them, and that's what they needed. And that's how God spoke to them.

However, there's a common phrase I've heard, and I said it to Blayn the night this happened to me:

"I don't know what it is, but I want more of it!"

That's how I know when people get baptized in the Spirit. If I'm not there, and they call me to tell me what happened, and they say that, I know. Typically, everyone says the same thing. And that's what I said to Blayn when she walked in from work.

I must have startled her because she stopped and said, "Whoa! What are you doing? Are you okay? What's going on?"

"I don't know what just happened, but I want more of it!"

Honestly, she probably thought I was on drugs again. But that's how God spoke to me when He baptized me. It was the best and it demolished and burned up every other drug that I'd ever done. It was like no other drug I'd ever done, no other drink I'd ever drank. It just totally and utterly destroyed it all. I don't have words all the way, but again, it was like electricity just shooting through me.

I shot up. I was telling Blayn all about it and she kept saying, "Okay, slow down. Slow down. What?"

Since neither of us had grown up in churches that preached baptism in the Holy Spirit, we really didn't know, either.

She tried to hear me out. She knows I'm real, I'm authentic. I don't fake things. She also knows I'm not hyper. I don't do things for show. Therefore, when she was hearing me and watching me, she was basically saying, "Okay, I believe you, number one. I believe you, but I don't know."

She called some people she knew, but they didn't necessarily believe in baptism of the Holy Spirit. Still, they said, "Okay, well, we know Bryn and he's not going to fake it." Basically, *he's authentic and if he said it, we believe him, but we really don't know*.

Therefore, at this point I didn't know what had really happened to me in that moment. Essentially, I had been baptized in the Holy Spirit and fire. God just poured His fire out on me and burned up everything that was not of Him that was still hindering me in any way. He set me *ablaze!*

That's where things really started to take off. It went from a slow grade to just shooting straight up. I still didn't know what I had received.

But I was about to learn.

6 Cleaning Up

"I indeed baptized you with water, but He will baptize you with the Holy Spirit." – Mark 1:8, NKJV

Out of habit and stupidity... ignorance, in the truest sense, I didn't know what exactly happened when I was baptized in the Holy Spirit and fire. Therefore, I continued to drink on the weekends.

I said before, I would only drink on Friday because I didn't want to be hung over for church on Sunday. Although I did that, don't think I was enjoying it. I hated it, every drink, every sip. I would start to get buzzed, realize what I was doing, and I would stop... and hate it.

I hated what I was doing, but it was a habit I couldn't seem to shake. Then, I would do it again. Each time I slipped, I hated it, I stopped, and I repented. Over, and over, again.

Finally, we were going to visit a friend of mine (not drug related) who lived in the Chicago area. I told Blayn, "Okay, this is the last weekend we drink. I'm done. I hate it. I don't even want to do it. I don't enjoy doing it."

I drank that weekend, only moderately. In my mind, I had gone from drinking heavily to moderately, and finally, I was done. Or so I thought.

A month later, I went to a bonfire, and, out of habit, I bought a beer. I drank one or maybe one-and-a-half. Somewhere in there, I became super convicted, because I told God I was done drinking.

I poured out the beer, cried, and I repented to Him. I haven't had a drink since. That was in September of 2020.

~

At this time, I still hadn't been water baptized. I was under the impression I needed to clean up my life first, like many people who believe they need to clean themselves up before coming to Christ, instead of just coming to Him and allowing Him to clean them up.

In truth, He had been cleaning me up the whole time, little by little. I wasn't taking credit for it, but it was partially out of ignorance, too, on my part, thinking that I had to come to Christ in this way for Him to accept me and to be honored. Not true.

In October 2020, I was water baptized.

I understand how people feel as if they must get their lives cleaned up to come to Christ, or for Him to accept them. I understand their heart because I was in the same place. It's out of fear and reverence for Him. We are taught that God can't look on sin. Therefore, in our minds, how can He possibly accept us if we're living in sin, regardless of what our sin is? But this is how the enemy tricks us, trying to keep us from the mercy, grace, and forgiveness of Jesus.

Therefore, to whomever reads this, you don't have to be cleaned up. Just come to Jesus. Let Him clean you.

I was praying and listening to the Bible, serving in church, and I was a member, trying to dive in more. I was baptized in the Spirit, I was saved, but then I was baptized in the Holy Spirit and fire – and then I got water baptized. It seems completely backwards, but that's how it happened.

I'm sure there will be people who don't agree, but this is how it happened for me. The point is not about the baptism in the Holy Spirit and fire. The point is that God took me, healed and delivered me, baptized me with His Holy Spirit, then began cleaning me up in a way that my life will never be the same.

I got water baptized in October of 2020. I quit drinking. Drugs were done. But things were just beginning for me.

In November, Pastor Jason asked the church to do something with prayer and reading the Bible every day for twenty-one days. So, I made the decision. I thought, *oh, I'm going to jump on this. I'm going to join.* When Pastor asked the church to do this, I wasn't reading my

Bible at that time.

The funny thing about this story is that I was praying here and there, not regularly, it was sporadic. But also at this point, I didn't know I was baptized in the Holy Spirit. I didn't know what it was.

I had no previous notion of what being baptized in the Holy Spirit was like. Even to this day, I don't want to say anything out of turn if God didn't do it. If He didn't tell me something, then I don't want to say it. So, I was hesitant. I didn't know what I had received. I didn't know I had baptism in the Holy Spirit, but I knew I was saved, and I knew that, in October, I'd been water baptized.

Therefore, in November, when Pastor had asked everyone to read and pray for twenty-one days, I started reading and praying every day. I have not missed a day since.

Through vacations, traveling for work, even when the baby was born, I have not missed a day. I'm not bragging. It's a staple for me. It's a priority.

This is where a lot of my spiritual growth has come. It's not in knowing His Word or airing my grievances. I have come to know God. I've come to know His heart. I've come to know what He cares about, what grieves Him. Part of that is the reading His Word tells you. Part of that is through prayer and communion.

It helps a person grow spiritually because we're supposed to be conformed to the image of Christ. We're made in His image, but then we've got to be conformed to His image. It helps to know the Person you're being transformed into their image.

Still, even reading through the Bible, I didn't know where to start reading, so I started in Genesis. I felt like, okay, this is page one. You read a book from the first page through to the end, so why not like this?

I started in Genesis and read all the way through. Then, I landed in a D-Group (Discipleship Group) at church and began learning more about reading the Bible.

Somewhere during D-Group, I began reading the Gospels. Now, when people ask me where they should start reading the Bible, I recommend starting in the Gospels. I feel it helps to understand things a whole lot more.

I was five months into my new life. In reading through the Bible, though, I still didn't know that I had been baptized in the Holy Spirit.

There was an older gentleman who came to our church, who was spirit-filled. I had started talking to him some, kind of getting mentored a little bit.

On my birthday (in 2020), he asked me, "Have you been baptized in the Holy Spirit?"

"No. Not that I know of."

I didn't know what being baptized in the Holy Spirit meant, entailed, how to receive it, or what it felt like, even though I had experienced uncontrolled tears, praying and prophesying, and felt electricity run through my body, burning up all the things I wanted to be done with. I was still clueless.

My friend prayed for me to receive baptism in the Holy Spirit. Afterwards, I was all pumped about it. I told Blayn, "I was baptized in the Holy Spirit!"

"Oh, that's awesome!"

"Yeah, cool!"

I went about everything the same because it just didn't click in my mind.

You can laugh here. Because when I was telling a friend about it, we had a good laugh. But isn't that how God is? He allows us to laugh, sometimes even at our own expense. It's so simple, and yet, all too often we miss it. But I'm getting off track.

I started reading the Bible more, and I was reading about people being baptized in the Holy Spirit. I heard people on YouTube because I was also listening to sermons throughout the week. Plus, I was reading other Christian books that were educating me further.

I listened to sermons where people would talk about when they were baptized in the Holy Spirit. I remember hearing them talk about it feeling like electricity was going through them.

Through reading in the Bible and then hearing other people share their testimonies, it started to click. *Oh! That happened to* me*!* Then it dawned on me, that had happened back in June. *That's* what had happened!

Still, I hadn't spoken in tongues.

The entire time, I was ignorant to the whole thing. When I prayed in tongues for the first time, I had asked people, "So, do you know when you're praying in tongues, or do you just think you're speaking in English and people hear it in tongues? Or do you know that you are?"

The answer was always, "No. You know."

"Oh. Okay. Does it just happen, or do you do it?"

"No. You know. You don't think you're speaking in

English, and it comes out in tongues."

The Day It Happened

I remember this vividly. I pulled up at work, because I always prayed when I got to work, which is funny now because back when I was using drugs, I would always do cocaine, and then go into work. Now, I pull up to work and pray.

I would pray in my truck. It was like my personal, private, prayer closet. On this day, I was praying, and I felt like I wasn't praying effectively. I felt as if I was just going through the motions. It felt like there was more to what I was needing to pray about, but I couldn't really put my thumb on it. I just didn't know.

The Bible says that when we don't know what to pray, the Spirit makes intercession for us. I thought, maybe I'm done praying. But when I went to get out of my truck, my legs didn't work. Literally. I thought, well, maybe I'm *not* done praying, so okay here we go. I'm just going to keep praying and I don't really know what to pray about.

That's when I started praying in tongues.

I didn't have a lot of words to put with it. I was going through those words, or sounds, however you want to say them, and it suddenly came to mind what I was supposed to pray about. I was supposed to pray about declaring any and every generational curse broken; over me, over my bloodline, specifically our daughter.

I prayed in tongues for a little bit, then that was the revelation that God gave me for what to pray. I prayed that in English, and then I felt a release and my legs worked again.

Afterwards, I got out of my truck and went in to work.

You begin to learn when God says you're done praying and when He says, *No, you need to pray more.* You can feel that release. That was the first time I really felt it and I understood.

After that, I started praying in tongues more. I would probably be lying if I said I prayed in tongues every day after that. However, back then, I did it more frequently. Now, I do it all the time.

Sometimes prayers don't come out the way we want. There are times when my prayers go from words, to tears, to groans, and sometimes ending up on my face on the floor.

Regardless, prayer is important. It's communication with God. In that, He talks to us, teaches us, and Holy Spirit intercedes for us when we need it.

7 "Why Do You Fear?"

"Don't be afraid, for I am with you. Don't be discouraged, for I am your God..." – Isaiah 41:10a, NKJV

I don't remember the exact date, and it really doesn't matter, but it was somewhere around 2020 when God audibly spoke to me.

I realize that many people either won't understand, or believe, what happened. But I know. I was there.

One morning, before work, I was preparing to go to the gym. It was dark outside, early morning, and a kind of worry came over me. I couldn't figure out what was happening, it was just a feeling that stayed with me.

I continued getting ready to leave the house, went out and got in my truck, and started down the road. I was halfway to the gym and, not in my mind, or my heart, but I audibly heard God speak.

"Why do you fear, Bryn, for I am with you."

I didn't know what to do. I usually drive with one hand, but in that moment all I could do was grab the steering wheel with both hands, stare straight ahead, and repeat, out loud and in monotone: *"Why-do-you-fear-Bryn-for-I-am-with-you."*

I drove in silence for the next five or ten minutes, staring straight ahead, until I got to the gym. I parked my truck and just sat there.

What in the world just happened?

I finally got out and went into the gym, and there was a certain presence that I felt, and I knew. I knew that God had spoken to me, audibly, and said that to me. To this day, I still vividly remember. It takes me back to that feeling. It took my breath away. I was in His presence, His glory, and I know He *audibly* spoke to *me*.

~

Fast forward a few years. I was praying in my office at work (I do that a lot at work). After a while I got up to walk down to the restroom, still praying as I walked down the hallway.

On my way, I was saying, "God, I just want to be with You." I was praying for peace because there's a lot of drama in the workplace, so I was praying about that, praying for Jesus to bring peace, praying to just be with Him, and be in His presence.

In the restroom, after washing my hands, as I was walking out, I heard His voice over my right shoulder, saying, *I'm right here.*

I felt as if He was literally right there, so I turned to look over my shoulder from where I heard His voice, and I saw a bright, white, radiant light. It was Him in all His glory. It was all I could do to not collapse on the bathroom floor.

I stumbled out of there and awkwardly held the door, as if He was coming out after me. Like, "Here, let me hold the door for You." I guess I was just trying to be respectful and hold the door for Him, even though I was completely undone.

I wanted to get back to my office, shut the door, and just bask in Him, in His presence, right there. When I finally got back to my office, that's what I did. I ended up kneeling and praying right there.

Later that day, I was riding in the car with my wife and family, and I told her what had happened at work.

"So, you saw Jesus?"

"Well, I mean, yeah basically. In His glory. It was kind of like the transfiguration on the mount, like how He became radiant."

"That's awesome!"

Shortly after that, in my heart and in my head, I heard Him again.

You've heard Me. And now you've seen Me. Now are you ready to live for Me?

Honestly, the first time I heard it – maybe part of the

first few times I heard it, I brushed it off. I truly thought it was me, or a voice trying to condemn me. So, I brushed it off. But then I heard it again. The same exact thing.

The Bible says, *"My sheep hear My voice, and I know them, and they follow Me." – John 10:27, NKJV.*

I know it was His voice. I know that I heard God. So, I quit playing these brush-off games.

I said, "Okay, God. I thought I was living for you. Am I not?"

There's more.

Then, He highlighted for me that ten percent (10%) was reserved. I wasn't all the way in. I was holding back, thinking, if things don't work, or if God doesn't do this thing, or if He doesn't come through, then I've got this to fall back on.

I was staying in my comfortability instead of just saying, "I'm all Yours, God. I'm stepping out one hundred percent. You say it, I'll do it."

~

Re-Baptized

I had been praying for a while about getting re-baptized but kept putting that off. However, in all the conversations God was having with me, I felt Him leading me to get baptized again.

It wasn't for remission of any sins, but because God hit me pretty hard with Joshua 3:5, *"And Joshua said to the people, "Sanctify yourselves, for tomorrow the LORD will do wonders among you" (NKJV).*

I felt that God was leading me to sanctify myself to

Him. It was like, hey, that ten percent is done. Are you all in? Then be all in; no more reservation. We're going for it. I would sanctify myself to Him, His will, His way, whatever He wanted to do in me and for me.

I was saved. I was delivered. I was completely changed. I had a whole new life, so why not get baptized again? Wash off all of that old life.

I had stopped the drugs. I had stopped drinking. I was one hundred percent sober. Therefore, I was sanctifying myself and consecrating the rest. Not ninety percent and ten percent. It was one hundred percent.

By this time, we were doing street ministry, working on planting a church, I was leading Bible studies, discipleship groups, I thought I was serving... well, completely. God showed me differently.

I think at some point, we all have reservation or hesitation, but that's not really what God has called us to do or to have. We are all guilty of that.

You know, no one has it all together. No one has it all one hundred percent for God. I know I didn't. That's why I feel He called me out on my reservation and compelled me to go all in, one hundred percent for Jesus.

And that's what I did.

8 Can We Skip the Big Fish?

"For if I do this willingly, I have a reward; but if against my will, I have been entrusted with a stewardship." – 1 Corinthians 9:17, NKJV

Understanding the concept of stewardship and how important that is to God should help us learn the importance of being good stewards of everything with which He has graced us. Essentially, it's all His anyway.

We went from doing outreach, moving to another state and city to do Bible studies and plant a church there. However, not long into it, we felt God calling us out of that place. We felt we were to plant a satellite church in the community where we had moved, but at one point it stalled. We didn't know exactly what was going on.

We would pray things like:

God, are You still wanting this?

Are we in Your will?

What is Your will?

You are God. If you will tell us to stay, we'll stay, and we won't regret anything. Just tell us what to do.

I had already had that conversation with Him, and He reminded me of Jonah. I said, "God, I'm here. I'll do what you want me to do, and I'll be happy about it. And when the people change, I'll be happy. I won't be upset like Jonah. I don't want to end up getting swallowed by a really big fish, just to end up where I was already supposed to be. So, can we just skip the big fish process?"

Blayn and I prayed about it for a few months when we felt as if God was calling us back home.

I heard three times, *Shake the dust off and leave*. So, we did, and we moved back. I don't remember exactly how quickly after we moved back, Pastor started preaching a sermon series out of Nehemiah, which was confirmation for us.

Nehemiah left his hometown to go work somewhere else. However, then he was upset about the state of his hometown, and God called him back to re-build it. Build and fight. He worked it all out.

Around that time, in my prayer time, I heard God say to me, *Compel*. Then He took me to look it up.

It's in Luke, the parable of the feast, where the master told the servant to go out and compel them to come in.

"Then the master said to the servant, 'Go out into the highways and hedges, and compel *them to come in, that my house may be filled,'"* Luke 14:23, NKJV *(emphasis added).*

That's where He took me. People heard and got invited, but they disregarded the invitation. They made up all these excuses not to go, and then the king said to the servants to go out and tell the lame, the sick and the poor, and all of them. Go to the highways and the hedges and compel them to come in.

That's how *Compel Street Ministry* got birthed.

We didn't know what we were doing. We just said, "Lord, You said it. We're stepping. You'll meet us there."

If God calls you, He will also equip you to do it.

God had called us to do street ministry. A group of us, who have a heart and passion for street ministry, go out once a week and walk the streets of a town, talking to anyone we meet, and tell them about Jesus.

We hand out tracts, the Gospel of John, and share the love of Jesus with people. We pray with people. It's a kind of old school method.

Our six-year-old daughter also had an idea to make and hand out *Blessing Bags* to homeless people, or people who are in need. These Blessing Bags contain everything new; deodorant, toothbrush, toothpaste, pack of baby wipes, underwear, socks, a blanket, and a $10 gift card to a restaurant in the area. Because of these bags, we have seen some cool things. But what amazes me is that the idea was inspired by a six-year-old. The

Lord is already working through her. She even colors them.

Being all-in, we not only do the street ministry once a week, but we are also involved in so many other ministries it's hard to name them all. In essence, we are off in the deep end, the deep water, with Jesus.

Therefore, when God said, *Now are you ready to live for me?* I thought I was! But He said, *Cast out in the deep.* It's His blood, my hands.

Now, I understand that's all deliverance by the finger of God. It's all by the Holy Spirit and His power. The same power that raised Christ from the dead lives in us. I understand it's not me. It's not by my might nor my power but by His Spirit. And I've seen all that stuff.

I was doing deliverance. I was laying hands on people and demons were coming out of them, even over the phone.

One day I got a call from someone. We were talking and suddenly the changed. So, I took it as if it was in person. Authority doesn't have to be in person. I remember the centurion who came to Jesus. He said to Him, *"Lord, I am not worthy that You should come under my roof. But only speak a word, and my servant will be healed," Matthew 8:8, NKJV.*

Therefore, we went into deliverance over the phone. It was interesting. I didn't have to see it. I could hear it.

I believe God asked me, and also asks you, *Are you ready to live for Me?*

What more can I do? What a question! I believe God says, *Let Me show you.*

I also believe God has said a lot of other things to

me since I said yes to Him; things about going further. If we are all honest, there's more that we have to give to God, surrender to Him, or live more for Him.

9 Sorcerer, Pagan, and then Revelation

"Before I formed you in the womb I knew you; Before you were born I sanctified you; I ordained you a prophet to the nations." – Jeremiah 1:5, NKJV

When I started working with my writing coach for this book, I learned some things about myself that I hadn't known before. I believe God showed me, and taught me, some profound truths which I also believe go unnoticed or unknown by others who struggle with addiction.

I walked into my meeting and blurted out, "Last

week I found out that I used to be a sorcerer!"

We laughed, and then I said, "I also repented for it this weekend."

She looked at me and said, "You were already delivered, though."

"I just wanted to make sure."

Again, we had a good laugh, but then, we became serious, and she asked me to explain.

I started studying out *Pharmakeia (pharm-uh-key-uh)* and the root of it.

Pharmakeia is in Galatians 5:20, Revelation 9:21, and Revelation 18:23. It means medication, or pharmacy, by extension; magic literally or figuratively. The sorcery witchcraft or enchantment, and the biblical usage is the use or the administering of drugs or poisoning or sorcery, magical arts often found in connection with idolatry and fostered by it, or of the deceptions and seductions of idolatry.

Pharmakeia comes from *pharmakeos (pharm-uh-key-us)*. It's in Revelation 21:8, meaning a druggist or a pharmacist or poisoner; a magician or sorcerer. So, the biblical usage is one who prepares or uses magical remedies, a sorcerer or magician, one who engages with occult practices would make up concoctions or drugs. Then, *Pharmakeos* comes from the root word *pharmakon*, meaning a drug or a special or spell-giving potion.

Pharmakeia refers to the practice of sorcery or witchcraft, often involving the use of potions, spells, and enchantments and is associated with idolatry and manipulation of spiritual forces through illicit means.

51

The cultural background in the Greco Roman world pharmakeia was commonly associated with the use of drugs and potions for magical or religious purposes.

Sorcerers and magicians were believed to have the power to influence a spiritual realm often for personal gain or to harm others. Such practices were prevalent in pagan religions and were condemned by Jewish and Christian teachings as they were seen as attempts to usurp God's authority and engage with demonic forces.

Therefore, pharmakeia is the use or practice of sorcery witchcraft involving drugs, so the act of using drugs, and then pharmacuse is the person or the sorcerer or magician who prepares or uses the drugs – also known as a drug dealer in modern day terms, and then pharmakon is the drug.

Apparently, I was also, unknowingly, into paganism, which I believe is part of the devil's greatest deception, if you're involved in drugs, you're also into all these things –sorcery, witchcraft, idolatry, paganism, and the like. I had no idea how I was a sorcerer. I thought I was a drug dealer. In reality, I was a sorcerer.

This is how drugs cast spells and enchantments on people. People think they do all these things innocently, thinking there is no spiritual connotation to it, or anything associated with it, but truthfully there is.

The revelation on pharmakeia is that if drug use is pharmakeia, meaning sorcery or witchcraft, then is addiction a spell or enchantment from the sorcery or witchcraft?

Yes.

It's been many years since my drug-dealing and

using days. God delivered me out of it all and set me on this path to serving Him. However, although the enemy has been exposed, God has been revealing more things to me, and the depth of exactly how far it all went – how deep I was.

Not only had I been a sorcerer, but a pagan. It was a mind-blowing revelation.

I got saved. But it was only on the surface. Now, years afterward, I'm finding out there's more and more for which I was forgiven and delivered. It's all under the blood of Jesus, of course. I know I was forgiven of being a sorcerer and all that, but when it was revealed to me, I went ahead and repented anyway. I wanted to cover all my bases.

It may sound funny, and we did laugh about it, but this revelation stirred me. What else had God taken care of that, at the time, I knew nothing about?

The same thing happened with paganism. I believe, as God reveals it to me, it isn't to condemn me, but so I have a better understanding of all He's saved me *from*, as well as the magnitude.

It allows me to be more grateful and thankful, and in a broader sense, to share to more people, to make my testimony more relatable. In sharing my story, God has helped me to bring understanding and insight to others, especially with marijuana.

The government does not legislate morals or morality. However, many people think that because they said it's legal, you can go buy it, then it's okay. But it's not. Biblically, it's not okay.

In the Bible, that's what sorcerers used; opium,

marijuana, cocaine, heroin, they used all of them to deceive people into thinking they were doing all these powerful, different things, but it was just a form of deception.

Now, we just have "legal sorcerers" selling marijuana on every street corner, out of dispensaries, that are labeled legal. No wonder America is where it is because they've condoned sorcery and witchcraft.

Sadly, they don't even realize it. All these people who go to the dispensaries are now under a spell, or an enchantment, of the drug. And all believe it's to help them manage whatever ailment or issue they're suffering.

Deception.

When people say, "Addiction runs in the family," they can all be generational curses passed down from one to the next. In truth it's a spell or enchantment that has brought on the generational curse, which needs to be broken by the blood of Jesus.

~

Created, Formed, Filled

Jeremiah 1:5 (NKJV) says, *"Before I formed you in the womb I knew you; Before you were born I sanctified you; I ordained you a prophet to the nations."*

I have since learned that we're created, then we're formed. We had to be created before we were formed.

It's through the creation story, also with Adam, that God formed the heavens and the earth, then He filled them with animals, with humans, and then filled even the sky with stars, the sun, and the moon.

Therefore, it's created, formed, and then filled. So, when we're all born, we're created in the heavens. Then, we're formed on the earth, in the womb. Upon salvation, we are filled.

I learned that I was going through life unfilled, which was leading me to be unfulfilled, because I had a void.

Because the earth was without form and void, it was not yet filled, but had been created. I've been created and formed, but I hadn't been filled because a person is supposed to be filled with Christ, with Holy Spirit.

Before my salvation and deliverance, I was going through life trying to fill that void with all these other things, alcohol, and drugs.

These things are fleeting. They would just fade away, burn away, and wear off. That's where a lot of it began, with me trying to fill a void with material things. I was coveting and then I kept going, which led me into needing more – more money, more things, etc. This led me into selling drugs, then trying to mask all these feelings, then cover up and fill this void with tattoos, drugs, and alcohol.

I had feelings of lack, insecurity… I was insecure in my life. As I was trying to fill those feelings, fill that void, I just spiraled downward until I couldn't go any further. I hit rock bottom. It was a pit that I just kept shoveling things into, that would never be filled without Jesus. That's when God began to work in me, then through me.

I used to be one of those unfulfilled people. I was

once where many of them are now. Hallelujah for salvation, forgiveness, and deliverance!

10 I Know What I am Not

"Therefore, if anyone is in Christ, he is a new creation; old things have passed away; behold, all things have become new." – 2 Corinthians 5:17, NKJV

In my new life, I know all the old things have passed away. They're gone. God has forgiven me, healed me, delivered me, and none of that old life remains, other than the tattoos.

I also know that many people won't, or don't, believe that, or accept it. Even in the Bible, there were religious leaders, and those who considered themselves religious, who just wouldn't believe, or let go of a person's past, or past mistakes.

Even Jesus experienced the unbelief and rejection of others. When He returned to Nazareth, His hometown, He was teaching in the synagogue and, although people were amazed, others were not.

"...Where does he get this wisdom and the power to do miracles?" Then they scoffed, "He's just the carpenter's son, and we know Mary, his mother, and his brothers – James, Joseph, Simon, and Judas. All his sisters live right here among us. Where did he learn all these things?" And they were deeply offended and refused to believe in him. Then Jesus told them, "A prophet is honored everywhere except in his own hometown and among his own family," Matthew 13:54b-56a, NLT.

Many people who come out of addiction, whatever that may be, are often labeled for life even if they've been delivered out of that lifestyle.

I have heard statements such as:

Once an addict, always an addict.

They're a recovering alcoholic.

Once an alcoholic, always an alcoholic.

I don't believe any of that. I'm living proof that once God heals and delivers you, then you are no longer what you once were.

I know what I am *not*:

I am *not* an addict.

I am *not* an alcoholic.

I am *not* a sorcerer.

I am *not* a pagan.

I am *not* unfulfilled.

I am *not* the person I once was.

Anyone who continues to try to put a healed and delivered person back into their past is going against Scripture. They are going against God's Word. They are going against God.

In 2 Corinthians 5:17 it states that if we are in Christ, then we are a new creation. Old things have passed away and all things are new.

"Therefore, if the Son makes you free, you shall be free indeed," John 8:36, NLT.

When Jesus redeems us, He also restores us. Our past is gone. Yes, we made some mistakes. Yes, we will make mistakes again; hopefully, not the same mistakes, but we are human and not perfect.

My question is, why did Christ die? Was it to leave us the same, or in the same mess, addiction, abuse, or in the same sin? NO!

Christ died to give us an abundant life, here and now, as well as in the life to come (John 10:10).

I know what I am not. But I also now know who I am, in Jesus Christ. I know my identity.

I am created, formed, and filled. I am saved, sanctified, and sealed. I am forgiven. I am *ful*filled. I am a new creation in Jesus Christ. I am redeemed, rescued, and restored.

I am also the righteousness of God, as well as a joint heir with Jesus. I am seated with Christ in the heavenlies. I am covered by the blood of Jesus. I am covered in the whole armor of God. I am a son of the living God.

I am a blood-bought believer. I am blessed with

every spiritual blessing in the heavenlies. I am the head and not the tail. I am above and not beneath. I am blessed when I come in and blessed when I go out.

I can go on and on about who I am in Christ. The Bible is full of those identifying markers. And even though there was a time when I didn't know who I was, when I was running and rejecting God, still He loved me. He chased me down, relentlessly. He never gave up on me.

I'm simply stating the truth. Therefore, if anyone reading this right now is experiencing backlash for making a mistake, or several mistakes, and if Jesus has saved, healed, rescued, redeemed, or delivered you, if you have completely turned your life around and you're living for and serving Him, may I encourage you now?

You are no longer who you once were. You are now a new creation in Jesus! Your old life is gone, and your new life has come. The Son set you free, so *stay free*! Do not allow anyone to put you back into your old life.

How do you do that? You make a conscious decision that you are going to live healed, delivered, saved, and free. *Daily*. The Bible says we are to deny ourselves, take up our cross and follow Jesus (Matthew 16:24).

Every day, we make the decision to stay in our new life, to stay living for Jesus, to stay out of that old way of life.

Is it easy? Not always. But then if we never had any struggles would we really be serving Him?

Jesus said we would have troubles in our lives (John 16:33). But He also encouraged us, reminding us that He has overcome the world.

~

Not everyone is going to understand my healing and deliverance. That's okay. However, God has used what the devil meant for my harm and demise. He took me from a slippery, miry pit of darkness (Psalm 40:2), showed me how demons were closing in on me, and how when I cried out to Him, Jesus rushed in and picked me up out of that pit.

The darkness fled in the Light of Jesus Christ. He held me like a child. He cleaned me up and set me on a firm foundation. He steadied me as I gained my footing in Him. He baptized me in His Holy Spirit and Fire, burning away everything that was once killing me, trying to destroy me, and He made me completely new.

Yes, I have a past. It's an ugly one. But it's also one that God has turned for good. He has equipped me so I can minister to others who are in the same lifestyle. I can now tell others how God delivered me, and that He wants to deliver them. He wants to deliver you. Regardless of your past.

It doesn't have to be drugs or alcohol. Whatever it is, Jesus can and will heal you. He will help you. All you have to do is cry out to Him and He will be there for you.

~

I can't end this book without one more miracle story from my drug days. I mentioned before about using cocaine. I am a big guy (if you've seen me you know).

When I was into using, I would do as much cocaine in one sitting as anyone else would do in a week. That's how deep I was in that world. I had done so much cocaine that I lost my sense of smell.

However, after my deliverance, one day I noticed I was picking up on an odor of some kind. In truth, I was *smelling* something. I quickly realized that could smell once again. In all the things which God healed me, He had even restored my sense of smell.

My journey has been full of miracles, signs, and wonders. Some of them are beyond anything I've ever experienced. My life is forever changed. God never ceases to amaze me with all the things He does in my life and the lives in which I'm blessed to be involved. All I can say is, when God changes your life, He does it big! Realizing who I am in Christ has been eye-opening. It's not over yet… but that's a story for another time.

Appendix A – Jesus Wants to Work in You, Too

Maybe you read this book out of curiosity? Maybe you read it to get to know me more? Maybe you read it because the cover stood out?

Maybe you read it because you are going through the same or similar circumstance?

Whatever the reason, I pray that Holy Spirit spoke to you through this, drew you closer to Him, and that you felt His undeniable love, grace, and mercy wash over you.

This isn't really about me at all, but what Jesus Christ has done in me, for me, and through me. It's really about what He wants to do in, for, and through you too. Maybe you aren't saved or find yourself going through the same or similar circumstance. I'm here to tell you that Jesus Christ loves you. He wants to show you who He is. He wants to set you free, save you, heal you, deliver you, and restore you! He wants a real relationship with you.

If you are going through the same or similar circumstance, I want to encourage you that if Jesus did it for me, then He will do it for you. The Bible says that the testimony of Jesus is the Spirit of prophecy meaning, if Jesus did it for one person, then He will do the same for others. Jesus is not a respecter of persons meaning He doesn't love one person more than another. So, again, I say if He did it for me then He will do it for you too! When the walls were closing and it felt like all hope was gone, Jesus came in, picked me up, and gave me hope and a future! Jesus Christ saved me, redeemed me, healed me, delivered me, and restored me, and He will do the same for you! Cry out to Him and let Him meet you right where you are, washing over you in His love, grace, mercy, and power as He breaks any and every chain that is keeping you bound!

Maybe you're not saved and feel God pulling on your heart as you read this. You can feel Him drawing you in closer to Him, showing you who He is. Revealing His great love for you! I want to encourage you to lean in now to what God is doing in you. Give yourself to Jesus Christ. Don't wait. Don't hesitate. Do it now. It's the best decision you could ever make!

If that's you then repeat this prayer out loud:

Jesus, thank You for revealing Yourself to me and showing me Your great love, grace, and mercy. I admit that I have sinned against You, and I thank You for forgiving me of all those sins. I believe in my heart and confess with my mouth that You, Jesus, are the Son of God. That You lived a sinless life, were crucified on the cross, buried, and resurrected 3 days later. I declare that You are my Savior and my Lord. I give You my heart, my life, and all of me, Jesus. I receive Your Holy Spirit and thank You that I am now a new creation! A child of God through faith in You, Jesus! Amen!

Hallelujah! Praise the Lord! Congratulations on the best decision you could have ever made on giving yourself life to Jesus! Heaven is rejoicing with you right now over your decision!

Here's my prayer over you.

Jesus, thank You for showing my friend who You are. Thank You for saving, healing, redeeming, delivering, and restoring them just as You did for me. Thank You for giving them a hope and a future. Now, Jesus, I pray protection over them mentally, spiritually, and physically. I pray that You would continue to draw them in closer to You showing them who You are. I also pray that they would continue to seek You and Your Kingdom first in all they do. I pray that You, Jesus, will ignite them with the same fire in which You ignited me. Holy Spirit I pray that You completely fill them, overflow in them. Light a fire that can't be contained or put out. Arise in them now! I pray they feel You doing it now in a tangible and undeniable way. In Jesus name, amen!

If you just gave your life to Jesus, want prayer, or have questions, then connect with me through email. I would love to celebrate your decision with you, pray with you, or answer questions you may have.

Brynedwards777@gmail.com

Appendix B – What is Tommy John?

Tommy John is an injury, or tear, to the Ulnar Collateral Ligament (UCL). The UCL is located on the inner side of the elbow which helps secure the elbow joint.

It is primarily caused by repetitive, forceful throwing motions, particularly in sports like baseball, where overhead throwing is common.

Repetitive stress can lead to small tears in the UCL. Worsening over time, it eventually can cause a rupture or complete tear.

Overuse is the most common cause, however, sudden injuries to the elbow can also occur and result in a Tommy John injury.

Named after baseball pitcher Tommy John, who was the first person to suffer from this injury. He was the first to undergo the surgery to repair the UCL and was able to return to his sport.

The goal of the surgery is to stabilize the elbow, reduce or eliminate pain and restore stability and range of motion.

This procedure was introduced in 1974, and first performed by Dr. Frank Jobe, M.D., on Tommy John, which ultimately earned the procedure its name.

Tommy John was a pitcher for the Los Angeles Dodgers in 1974, where he injured his UCL. After his successful reconstructive surgery, and subsequent rehabilitation, he recovered well and was able to return to MLB.

In 1977, after his incredible recovery and return, including a 20-win season, Tommy John earned the nickname, The Bionic Man.

For more information on the Tommy John injury and procedure, you can visit Johns Hopkins Medicine at www.hopkinsmedicine.org, Raleigh Surgery Center at www.raleighsurgerycenter.com, or the Cleveland Clinic at www.my.clevelandclinic.org.

Appendix C – About the Cover

A lot of thought and planning went into this cover – and maybe a little bit of mischief. With the help of my writing coach, and cover creator, who were both more than helpful in seeing this book realized. They listened, gave advice, brainstormed ideas, and let me know when they thought something would or would not work. But through it all, they were professional and supportive of this project.

My idea for this cover came out of what God delivered me: being a drug addict and dealer. I wasn't concerned with what others would think of me, rather, I was more concerned about putting the message of deliverance out there to people who are searching for a way out of the lifestyle of drugs – the right way.

I wanted to convey a message of hope and healing with the cover of this book. Therefore, what you hold in your hands is what my team and I came up with. But there is more to the cover than just what you can see with your eye.

Cocaine Bricks: This symbolizes the dark world from which God literally delivered and saved me.

Lightning Bolt: Lightning symbolizes God's authority and power, as well as His glory, presence, and judgment.

White Brick Wall: We chose white bricks because white represents purity and holiness. The bricks represent reliability, trustworthiness, and strength.

White: Spiritually, the color white is associated

with truth, purity, cleansing, healing, holiness, and righteousness.

Gold: symbolizes God's glory, divine presence, holiness, and divine favor. Gold is incorruptible.

Endnotes

Foreword *by Jason McKinnies*
Psalms 142, New Living Translation
Numbers 6:24-26, New Living Translation

Introduction
Acts 2, New Living Translation
Acts 1:5-8, New Living Translation

In the Beginning

Making the Connection
John 10:10, New King James Version

No Such Thing as Luck

God, Help Me!
Psalms 46:1, New King James Version

Savior, But Not Lord
Psalms 18:2a, New Living Translation

Cleaning Up
Mark 1:8, New King James Version

"Why Do You Fear?"
Isaiah 41:10a, New King James Version
John 10:27, New King James Version
Joshua 3:5, New King James Version

Can We Skip the Big Fish?
1 Corinthians 9:17, New King James Version
Story of Jonah in the book of Jonah
"Shake the dust off" reference in Matthew 10:14, Mark 6:11, Luke 9:5, and Acts 13:51
Reference to Nehemiah, chapter 4
Luke 14:23, New King James Version
Matthew 8:8, New King James Version

Sorcerer, Pagan, and then Revelation
Jeremiah 1:5, New King James Version
References to Galatians 5:20, Revelation 9:21, and Revelation 18:23
Jeremiah 1:5, New King James Version
Pharmakeia, pharmakon, pharmaeus definitions from Blue Letter Bible and Bible Hub
www.blueletterbible.com
www.biblehub.com

I Know What I am *NOT*
2 Corinthians 5:17, New King James Version
Matthew 13:54b-56a, New Living Translation
John 8:36, New Living Translation
References to John 10:10, Matthew 16:24, John 16:33, and Psalms 40:2

Appendix A
God Wants to Work in You, Too

Appendix B
What is Tommy John?

Johns Hopkins Medicine
www.johnshopkinsmedicine.org
Raleigh Surgery Center
www.raleighsurgerycenter.com
Cleveland Clinic
www.my.clevelandclinic.org

Appendix C
About the Cover

About the Author

Bryn Edwards is a process improvement engineer who works in the manufacturing industry.

After his salvation and deliverance from a life of drugs and alcohol, Bryn also, reluctantly, stepped into the literary world to write his story, in the hopes of helping others.

Bryn lives in Southern Illinois with his wife, Blayn.

Together they have two children, Quynn and Banner.

When they aren't doing street ministry, Bryn and Blayn can be found organizing baptisms at their church, praying for others, as well as leading Bible studies and discipleship groups.

Ever the entrepreneur, Bryn, along with Blayn, recently launched a new clothing business, *That's My King*. Their heart is to use clothing with a message to continue to tell people about the love of Jesus.

You can connect with Bryn at the following link:

Website: www.thatsmykingco.com

Bryn and his family.
L to R: Blayn, holding Banner.
Quynn, held by Bryn.

Coming in 2026!

I Am Because He Said
Understanding Your Identity in Christ

As followers of Jesus, it's important for us to know who we are in Him.

We are not defined by our circumstances, past, mistakes, or what others say to and about us. When we accept Jesus Christ as Lord and Savior, He gives us a new identity in Him; the old things are gone, and the new life has begun.

Bryn Edwards dives deep into Scripture to take an in-depth look at our identity in Christ, according to the Word of God. Using biblical truths, he dispels the myths and the lies of the enemy to bring forth identity in Christ in a fresh and uplifting way.

I Am Because He Said releases in fall of 2026.

Published by That's My King Publishing

www.ingramcontent.com/pod-product-compliance
Lightning Source LLC
Chambersburg PA
CBHW031243120626
46545CB00007B/2628